The One with All the
COLORING

Published in the United States by:
ULYSSES PRESS
P.O. Box 3440
Berkeley, CA 94703
www.ulyssespress.com

ISBN: 978-1-64604-164-0

5 7 9 10 8 6 4
Printed in Canada by Marquis Book Printing

The One with All the COLORING

An Unofficial Coloring Book for Fans of *Friends*

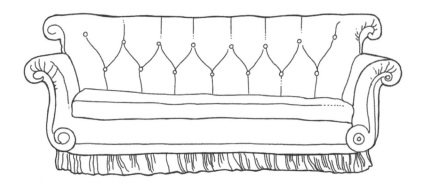

Illustrated by Valentin Ramon

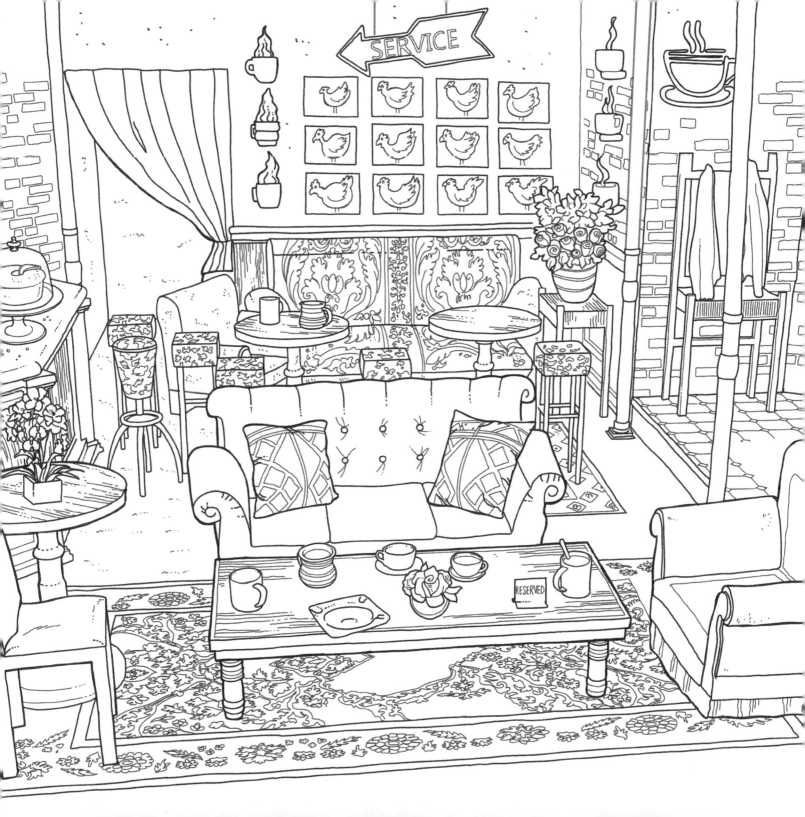

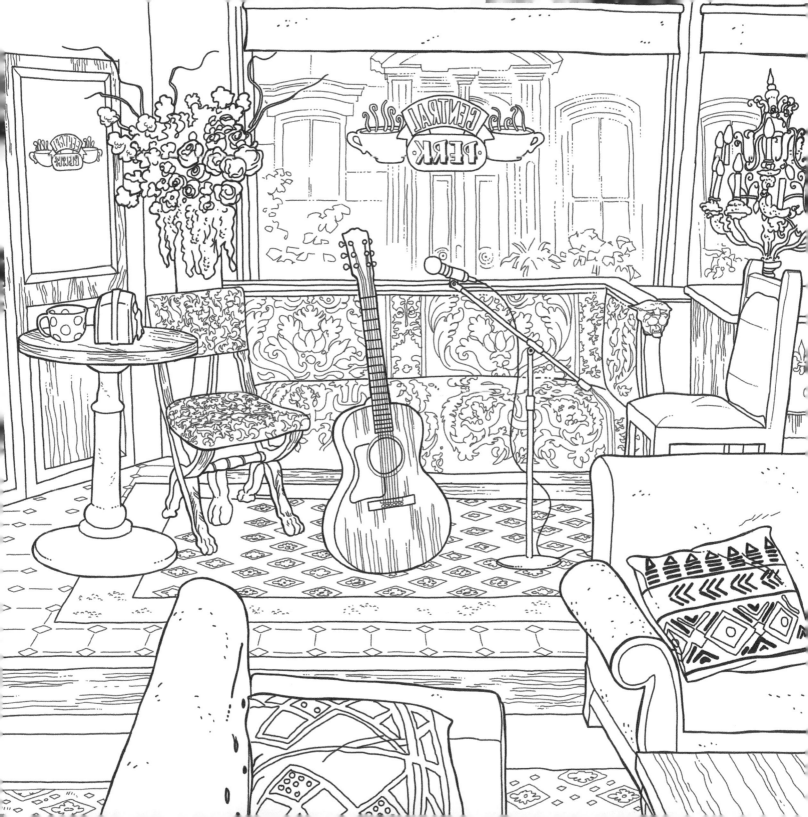

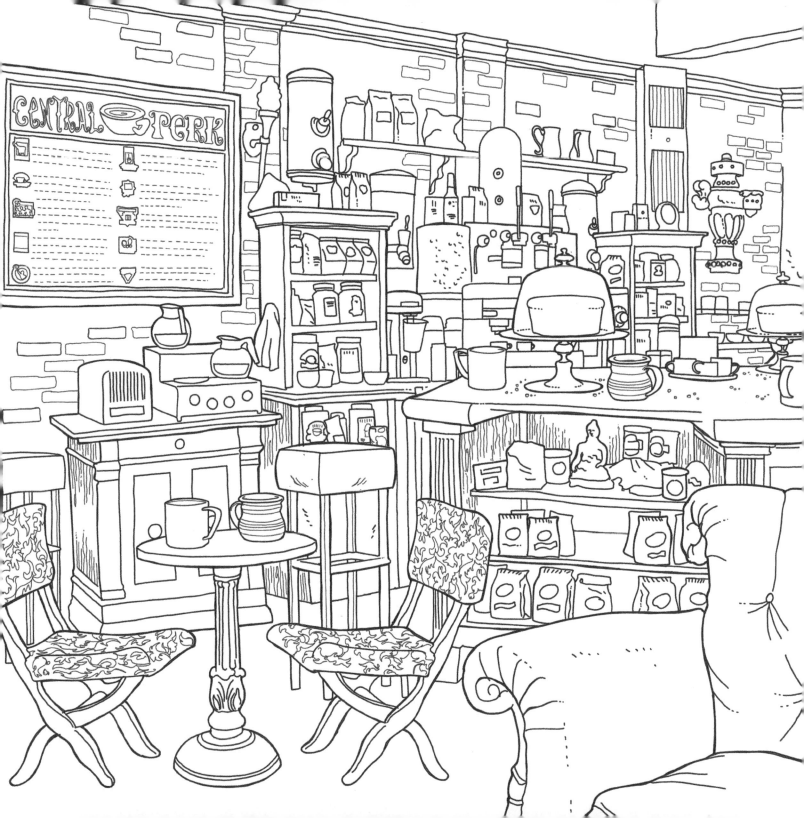

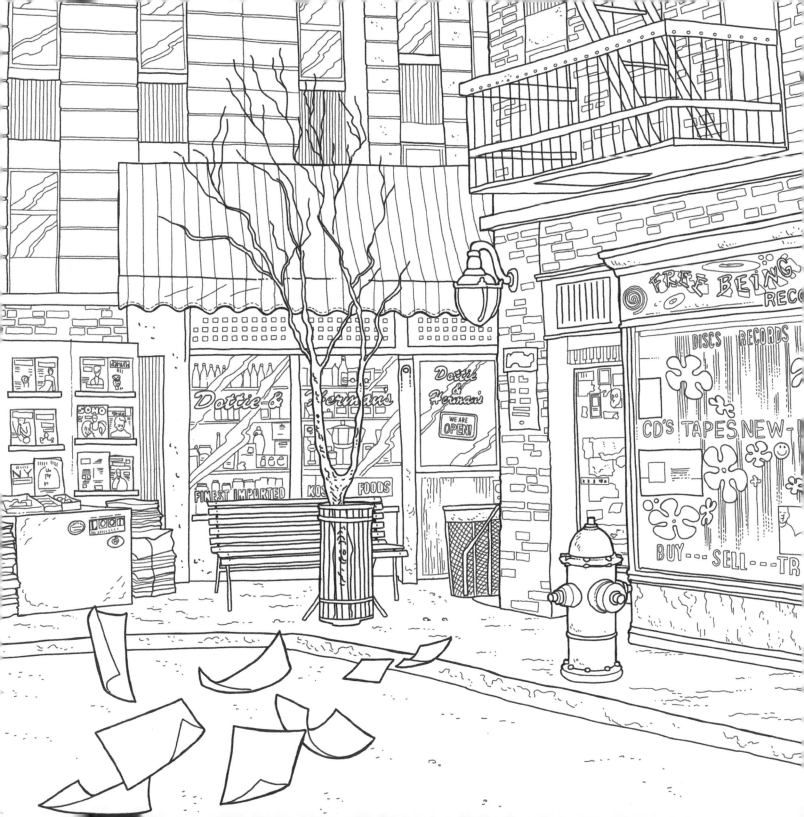

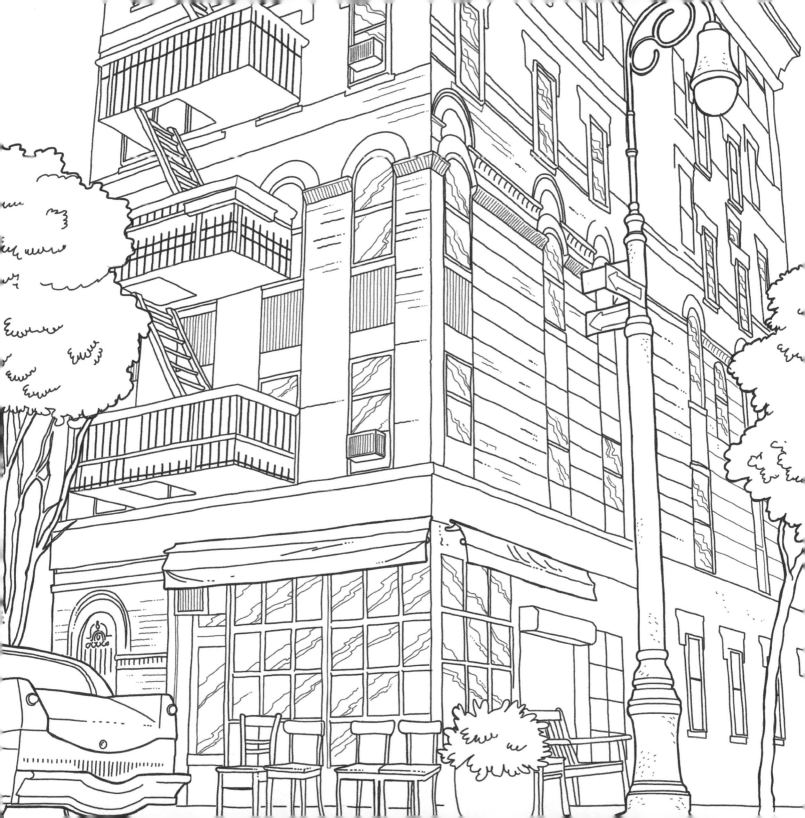

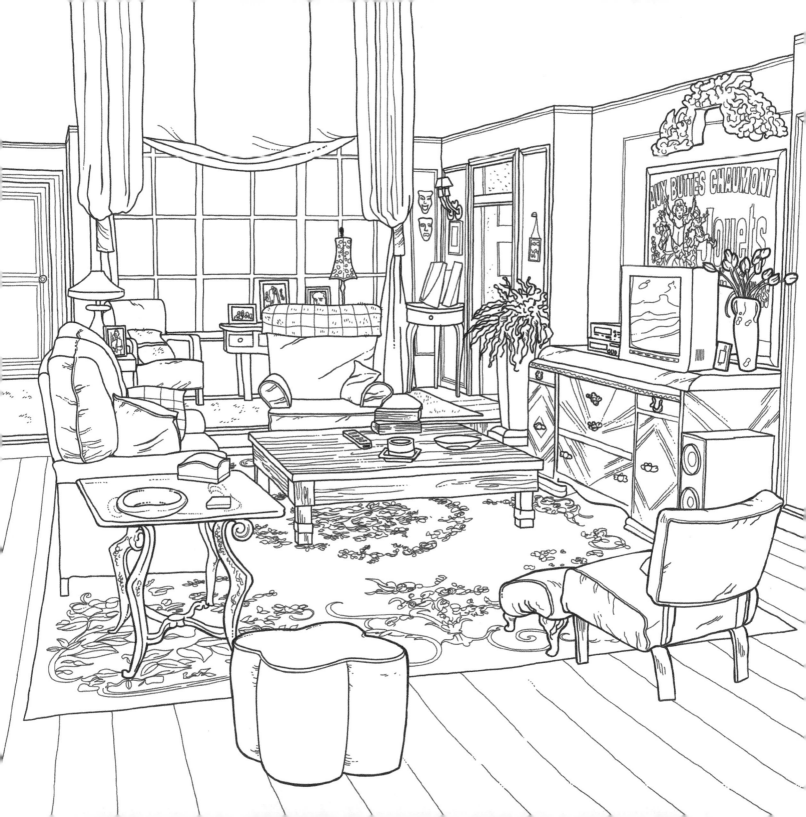

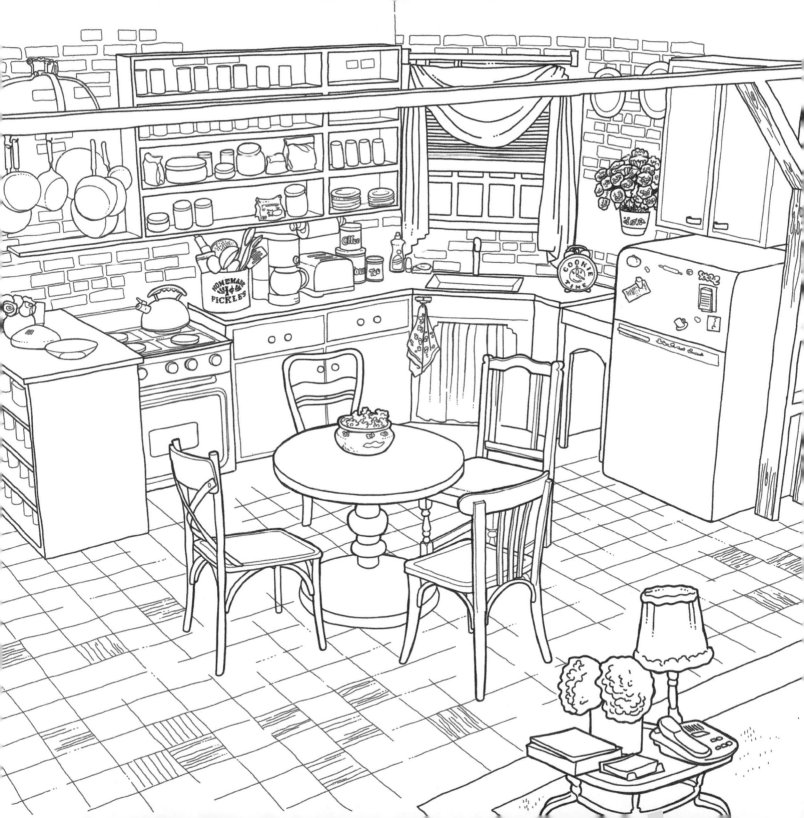

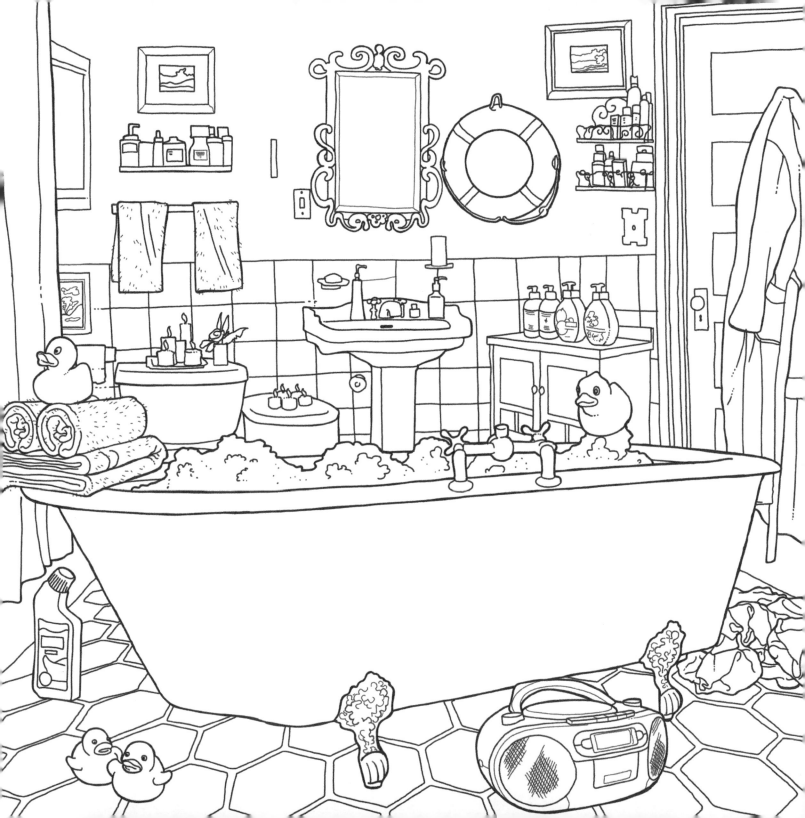

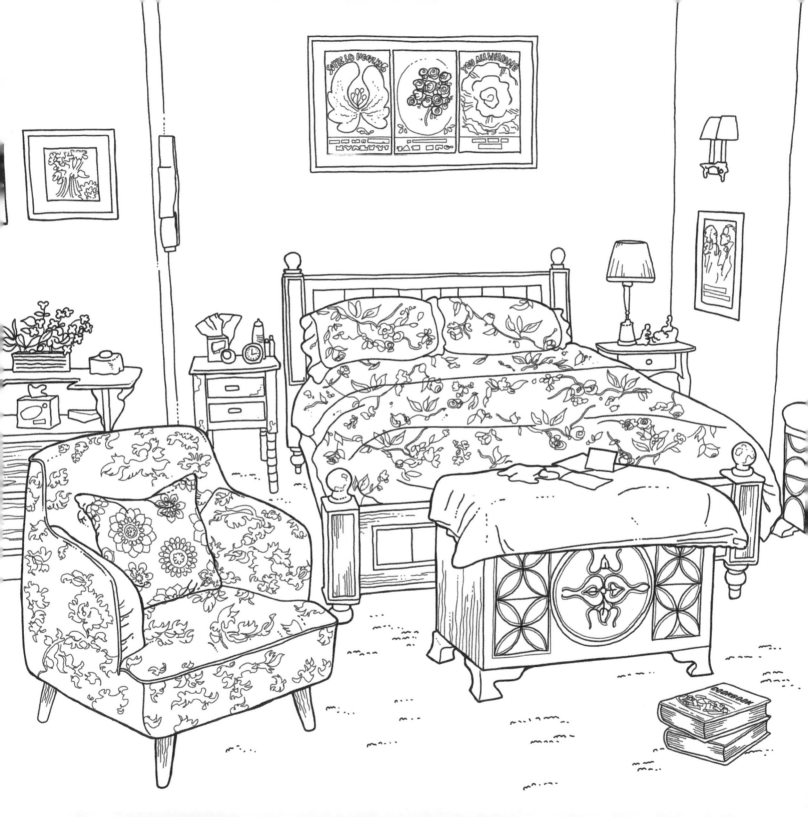

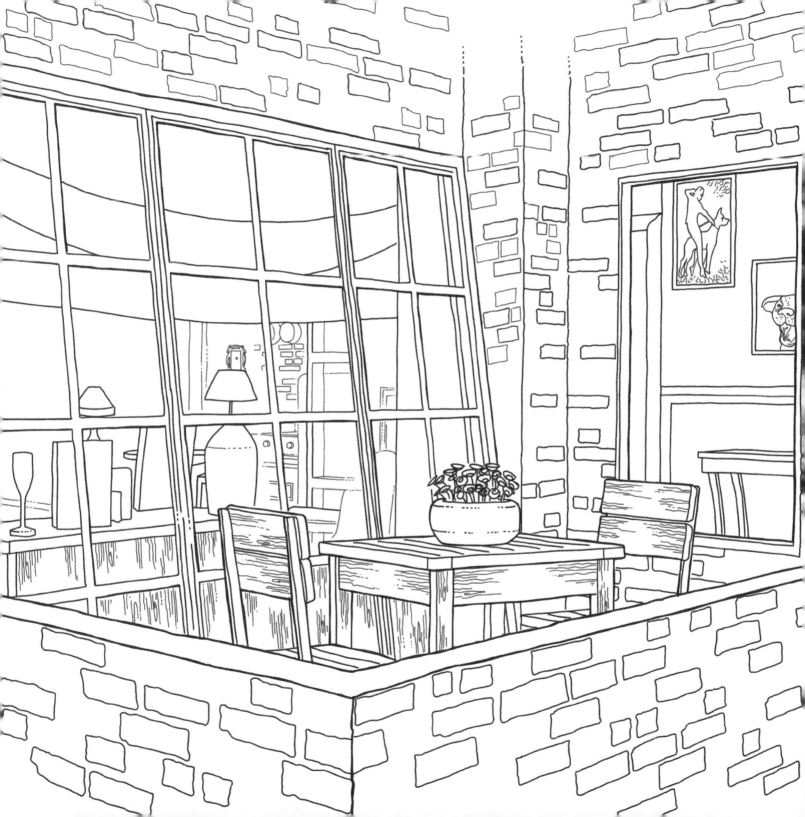

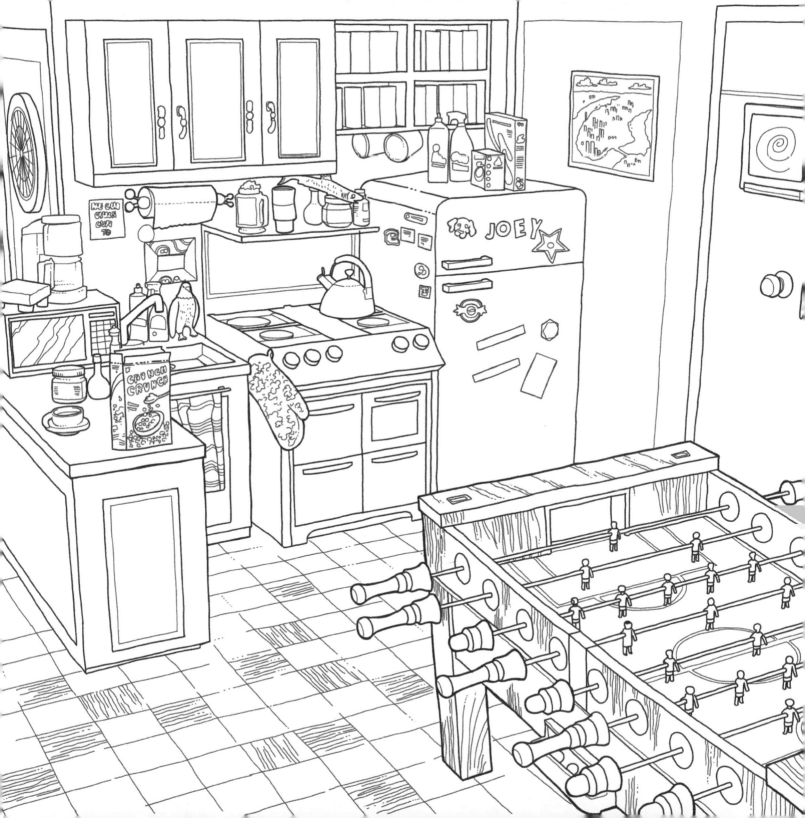

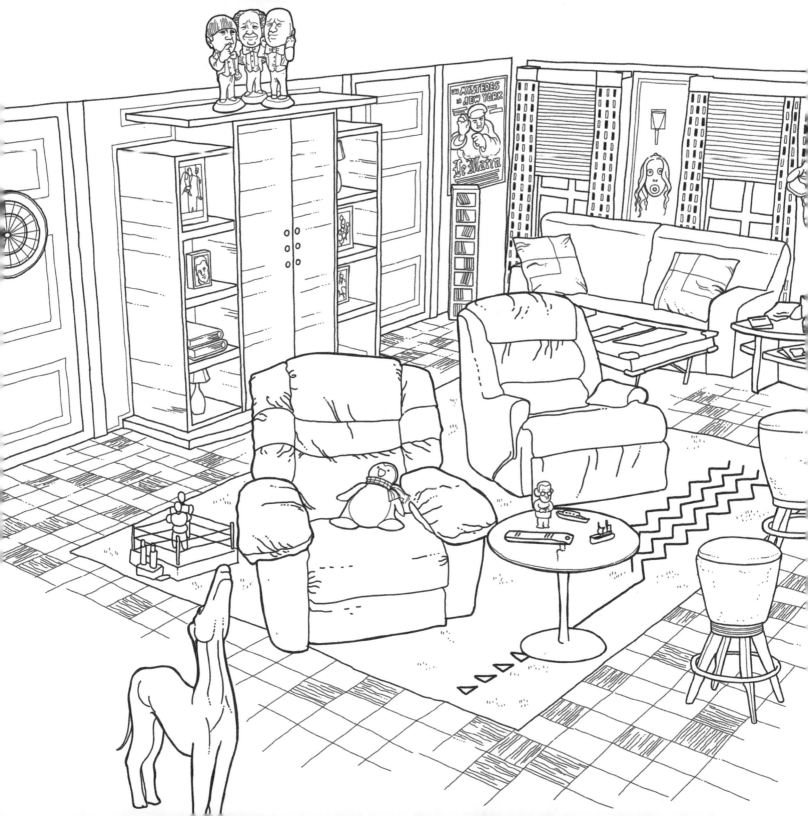

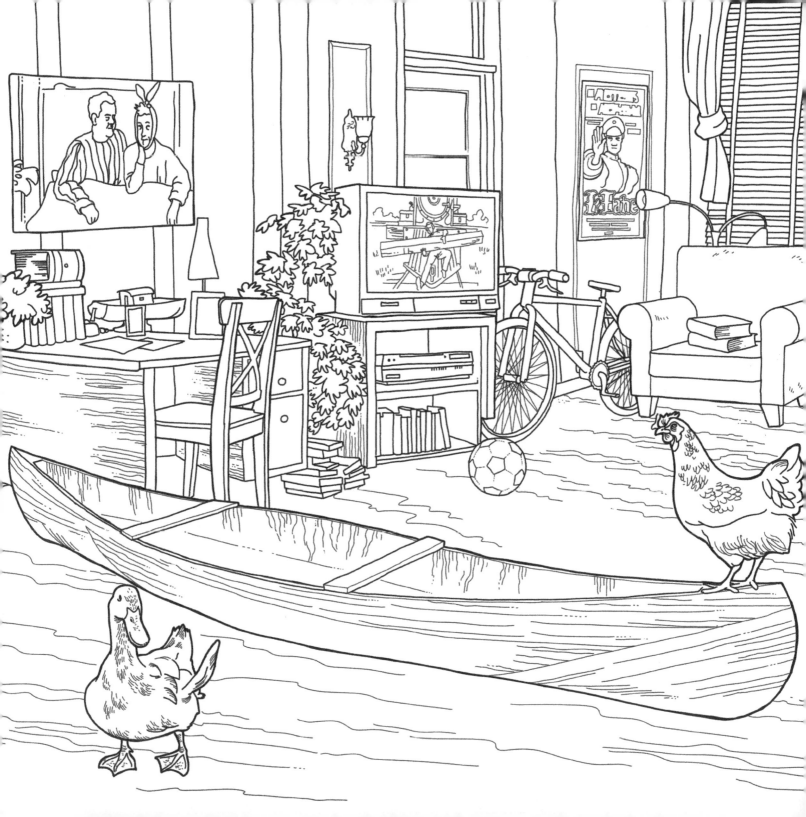

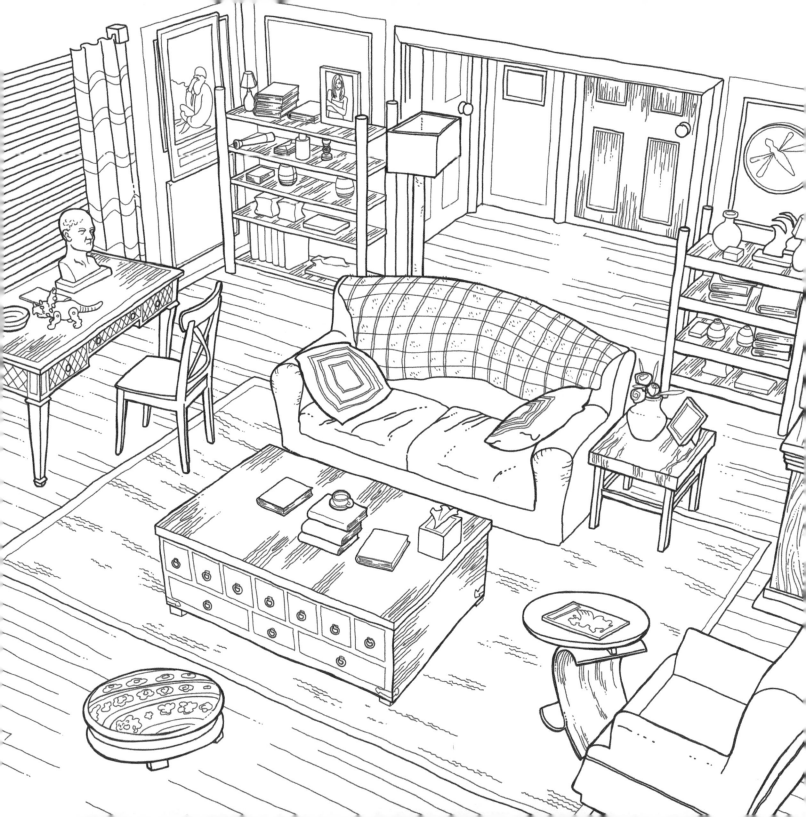

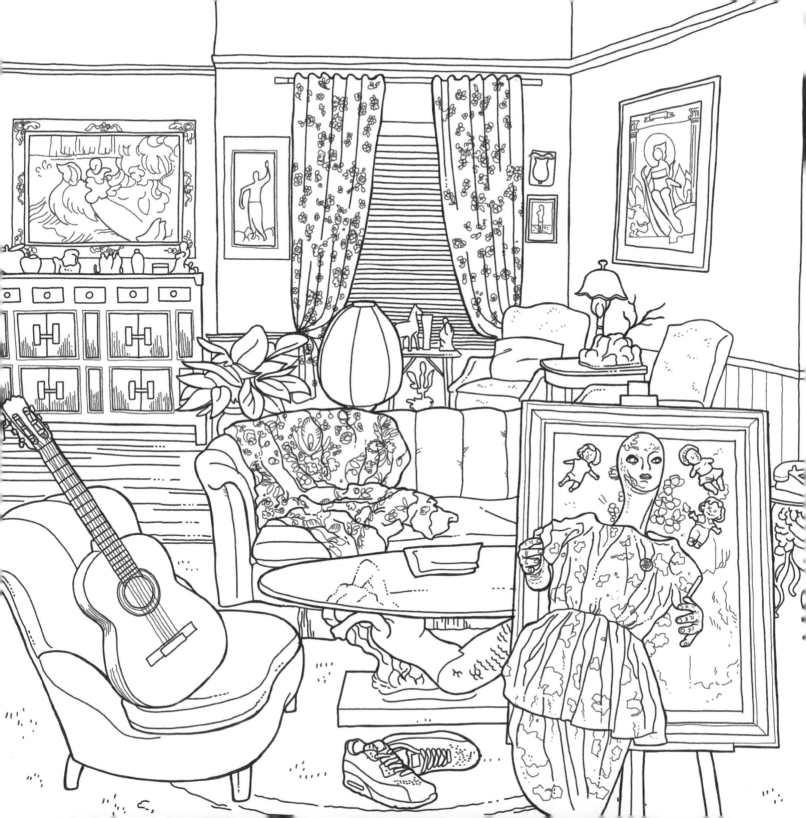

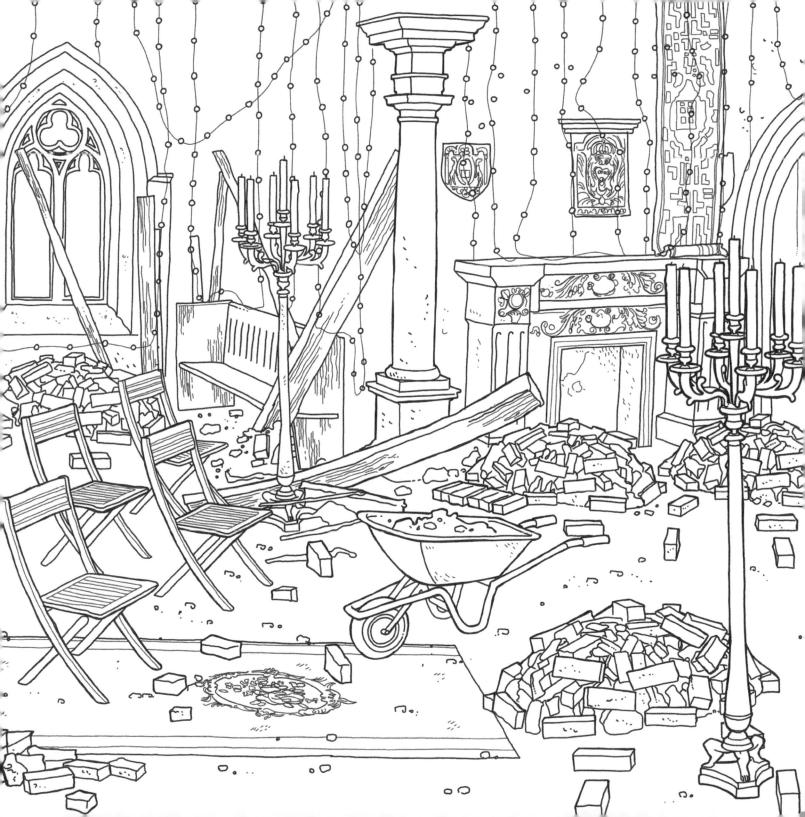

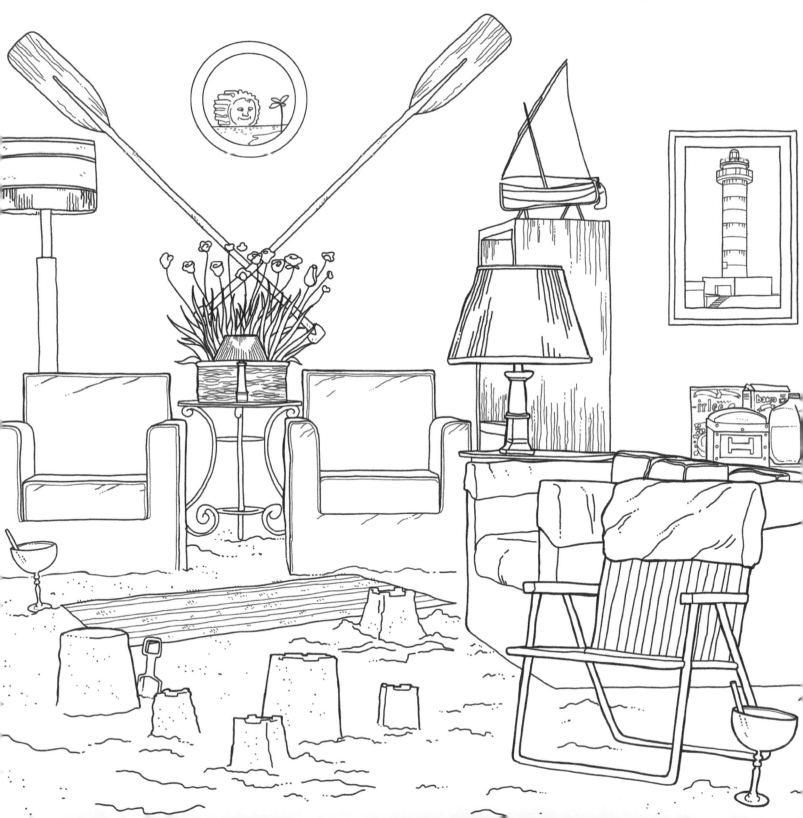

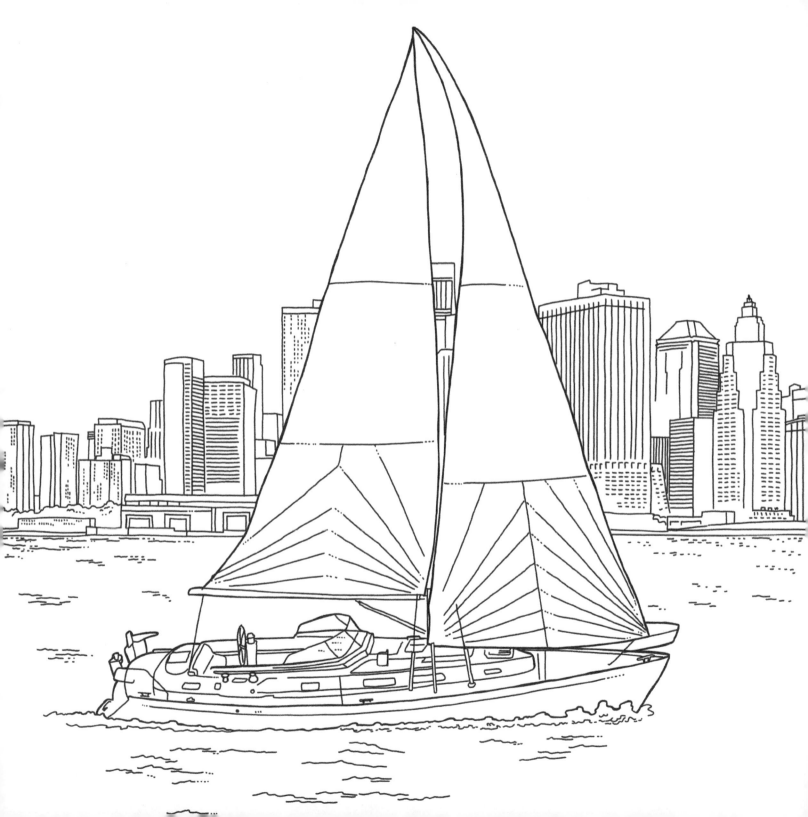

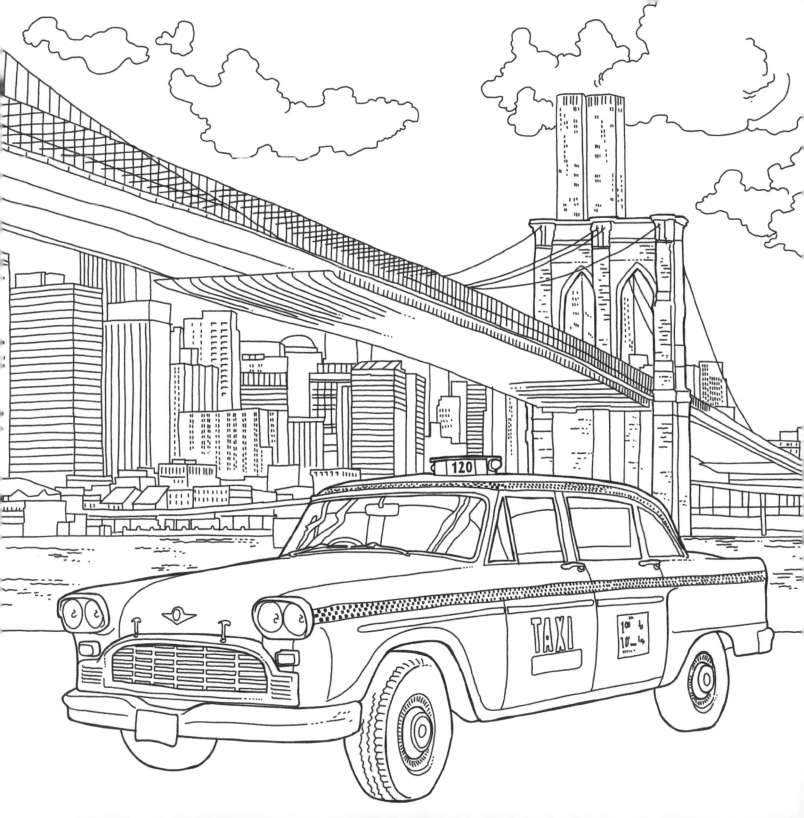

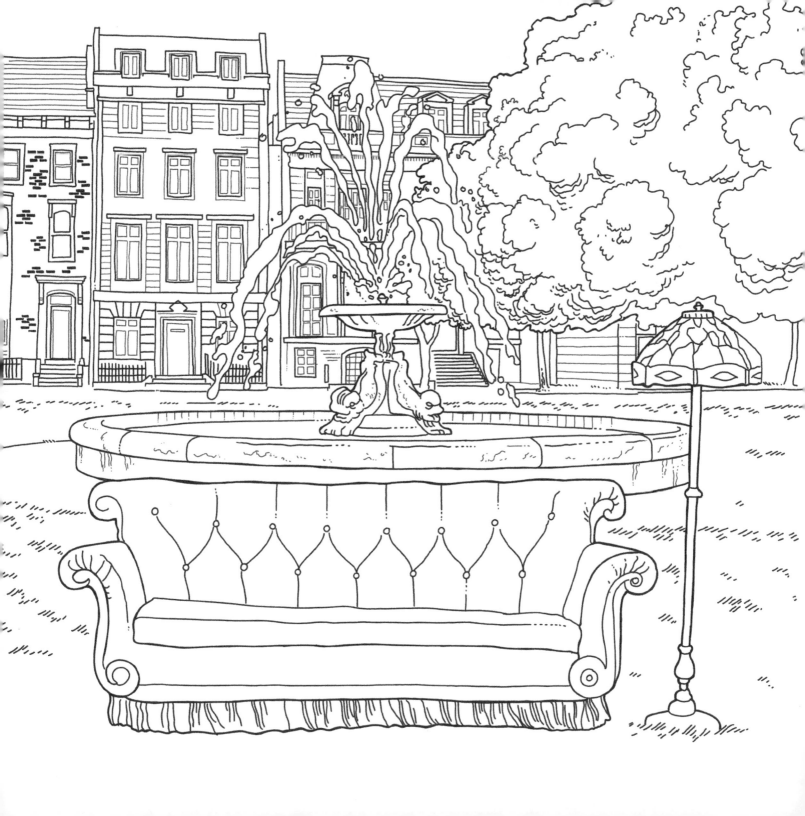

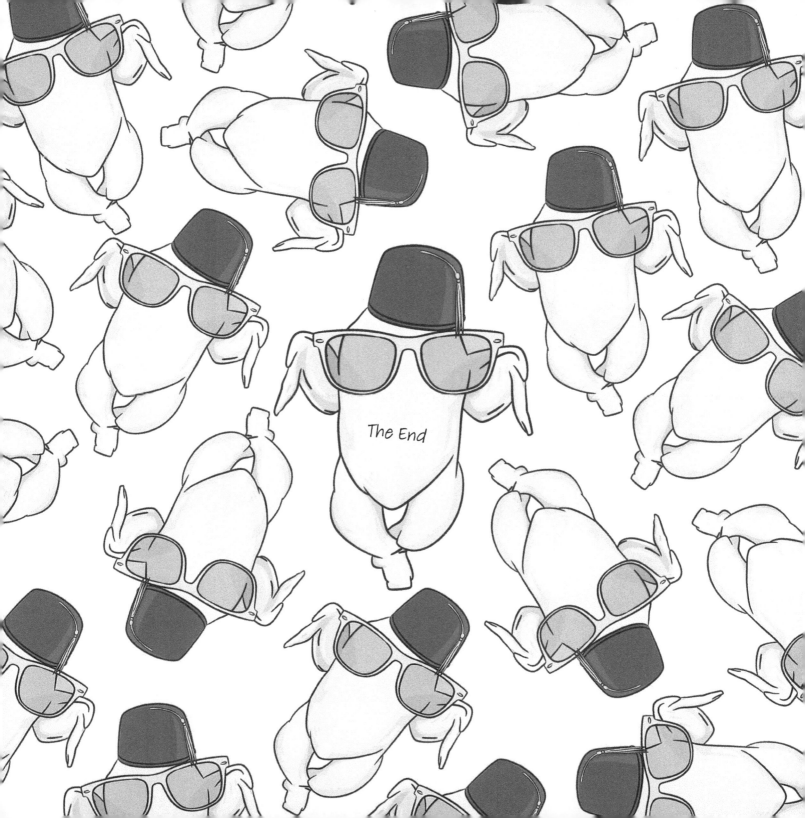

The End

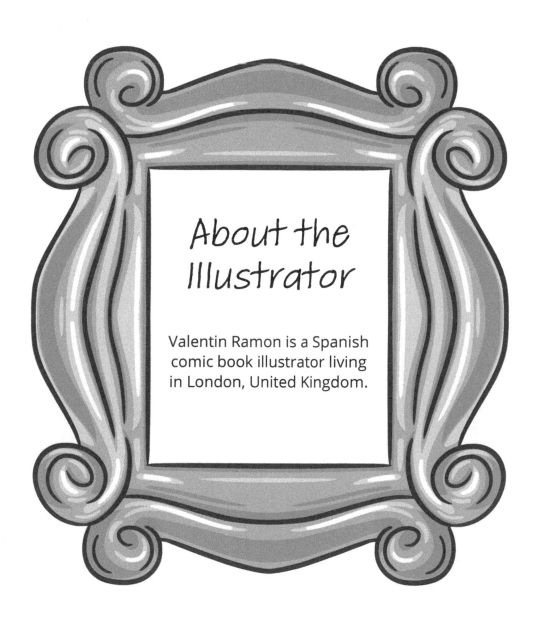

About the Illustrator

Valentin Ramon is a Spanish comic book illustrator living in London, United Kingdom.

Discover More Books for Fans of Friends

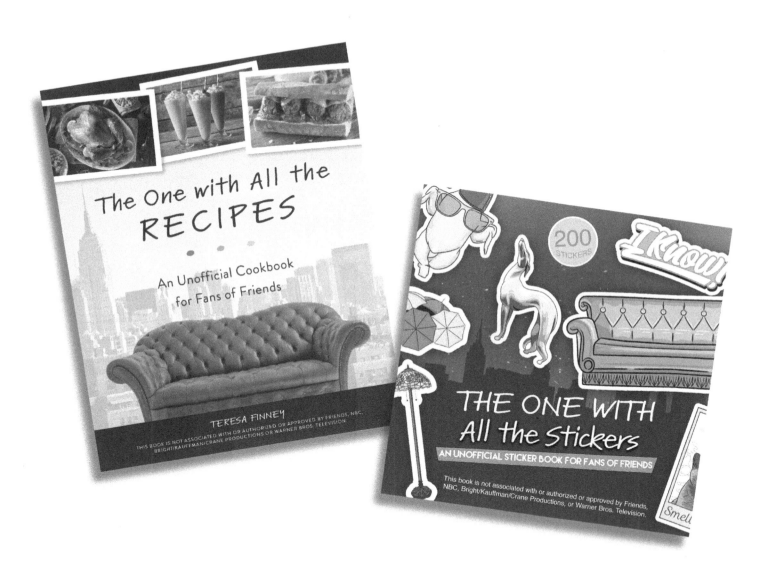